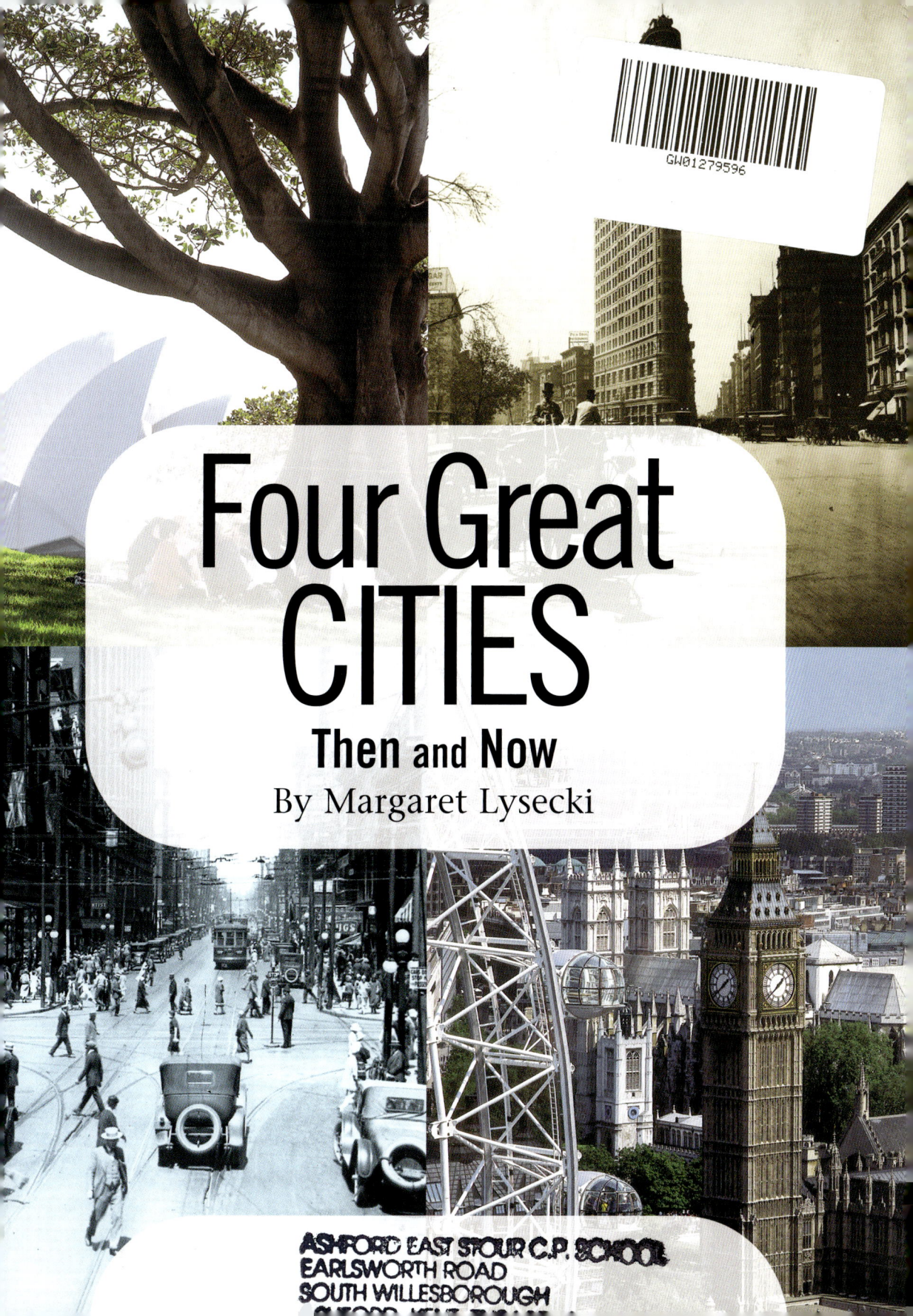

Four Great CITIES

Then and Now

By Margaret Lysecki

Series Literacy Consultant
Dr Ros Fisher

Pearson Education Limited
Edinburgh Gate
Harlow
Essex CM20 2JE
England

www.longman.co.uk

The rights of Margaret Lysecki to be identified as the author of this Work have been asserted by her in accordance with the Copyright, Designs and Patents Act, 1988.

Text Copyright © 2004 Pearson Education Limited. Compilation Copyright © 2004 Dorling Kindersley Ltd. All rights reserved. No part of this publication may be reproduced, stored in a retrieval system or transmitted in any form or by any means electronic, mechanical, photocopying, recording, or otherwise, without either the prior written permission of the publishers and copyright owners or a licence restricted copying in the United Kingdom issued by the Copyright Licensing Agency Ltd., 90 Tottenham Court Road, London W1P 9HE

ISBN 0 582 84135 6

Colour reproduction by Colourscan, Singapore
Printed and bound in China by Leo Paper Products Ltd.

The Publisher's policy is to use paper manufactured from sustainable forests.

The following people from **DK** have contributed to the development of this product:

Art Director Rachael Foster
Martin Wilson **Managing Art Editor** | **Managing Editor** Marie Greenwood
Kath Northam **Design** | **Editorial** Jennie Morris
Helen McFarland **Picture Research** | **Production** Gordana Simakovic
Richard Czapnik, Andy Smith **Cover Design** | **DTP** David McDonald
Consultant David Green

Dorling Kindersley would like to thank: Shirley Cachia and Rose Horridge in the DK Picture Library; Ed Merritt in DK Cartography; Johnny Pau for additional cover design work; and Mariana Sonnenberg for additional picture research.

Picture Credits: Alamy Images: Dominic Burke 9b; Don Jon Red 7tl; Felix Stensson 23tr. Corbis: 11tl; David Ball 24-25; Bettmann 5bc, 9t, 10; Hulton-Deutsch Collection 4br, 20ca; Scott Houston 15br; Hurewitz Creative 17; Louis K. Meisel Gallery 16cr; Schenectady Museum; Hall of Electrical History Foundation 5tcr, 14b; Paul A. Souders 27br; Underwood & Underwood 1tr, 1bl, 2, 4tr, 22; Ron Watts 20-21; Chad Weckler 12-13; The Brett Weston Archive 16b; Michael S. Yamashita 13t. DK Images: Mitchell Library, State Library of New South Wales 28tl. Mary Evans Picture Library: 8, 15bl. Getty Images: Hulton Archive /Fox Photos 27bl, 28b. Masterfile UK: Rommel 23cbr. National Library of Australia: 26. Photolibrary.com: 6-7, 23cbl. Reuters: Andrew Wallace 21b. Getty Images: Paul Souders 25tr; Space Frontiers /Taxi 45,c. Cover: Hulton Archive/Getty Images: front bl. Masterfile UK: Lloyd Sutton front t.

All other images: DK Dorling Kindersley © 2004. For further information see www.dkimages.com
Dorling Kindersley Ltd., 80 Strand, London WC2R 0RL

Contents

A Changing World — 4

London: Ancient Port to Modern City — 6

New York: Small Island to Metropolis — 12

Toronto: "Meeting Place" to Thriving City — 18

Sydney: Convict Settlement to Olympic City — 24

Appendix: Fast Facts — 30

Glossary — 31

Index — 32

A Changing World

During the 20th century, the world population grew from fewer than 2 billion to more than 6 billion. In 1900 almost all of the world's population lived in rural areas. By 2000 more than half of all people lived in urban areas, or cities.

Over the years, the great movement of people into cities has presented many challenges. People in cities now have an increased demand for food, housing, clothing, goods and employment. Transport is often difficult as well, because so many people have to travel from one place to another. All cities face the problem of meeting such needs. However, people in cities have done a remarkable job, working together to overcome these challenges.

On the following pages, you will read about four cities: London, New York, Toronto and Sydney. You will discover how these cities have changed over the past hundred years and how each city has become a great **metropolis**.

Toronto, Canada

London, United Kingdom

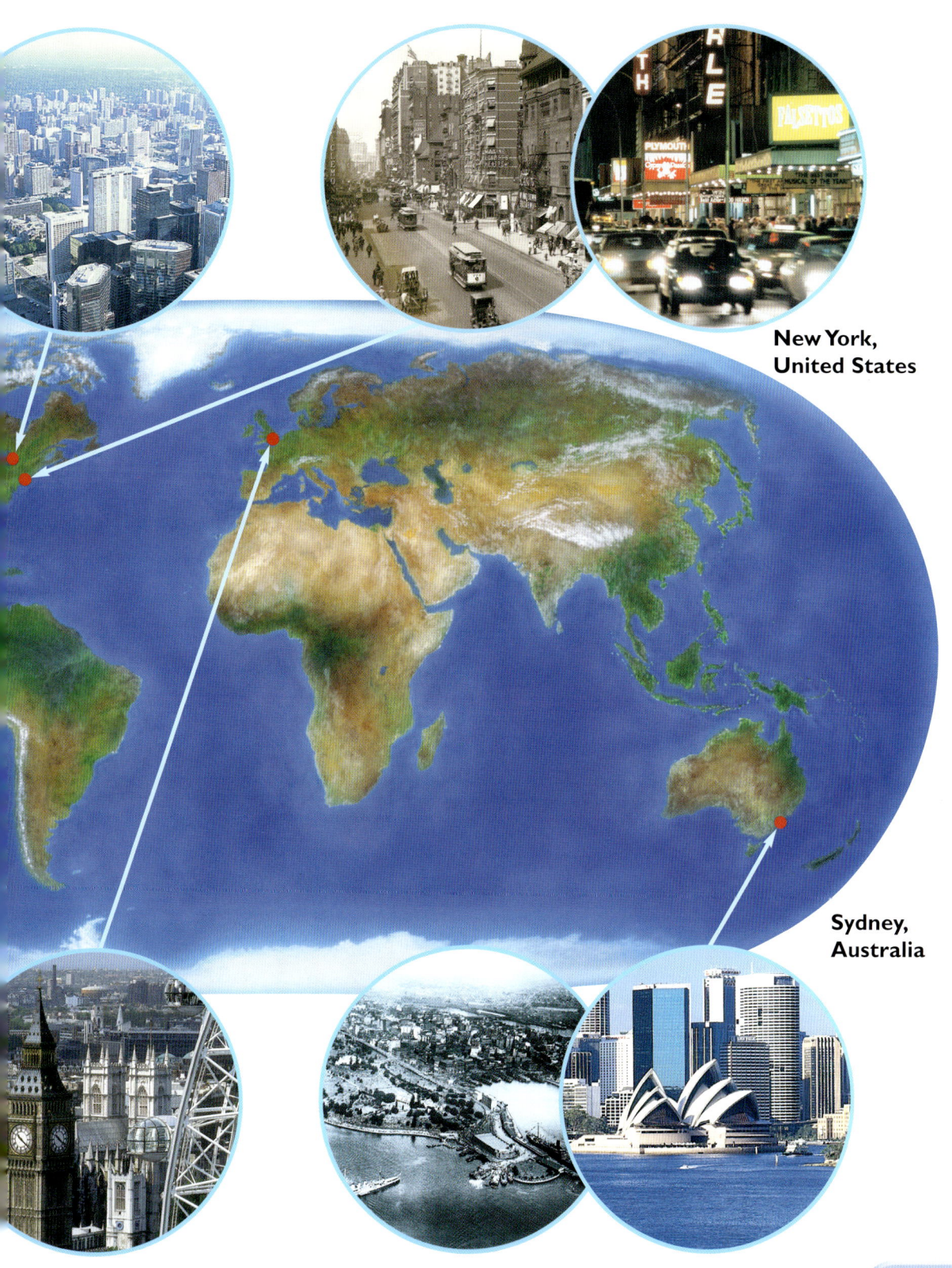

New York,
United States

Sydney,
Australia

London
Ancient Port to Modern City

About 2,000 years ago, the city of London was a Roman port on the River Thames. By the 1900s London was a huge city. Its port had become a busy place to **import** and **export** goods. London had many successful workshops, factories and businesses. Many people moved to London for work. Its built-up area soon spilled over into the surrounding countryside. In 1900 this vast **metropolitan area**, known as Greater London, had a population of 6 million and covered an area of 1,600 square kilometres.

By the end of the 20th century, Greater London's port area continued to thrive as a centre for importing and exporting goods. By 2001 the population of Greater London had reached almost 7.2 million.

Londoners

In the early 1800s most people in the United Kingdom lived in the country. However, by 1900 more than three-quarters of the population lived in cities or towns. About a sixth of these people lived in London and the surrounding areas. Many people came from rural areas to work in the city. Others came from overseas.

People from Ireland flocked to London during the Great Potato Famine that lasted from 1845 to 1849. Large numbers of Jewish people arrived in the late 1800s. After World War II thousands **emigrated** from the West Indies, Asia, Africa and the Middle East. These new Londoners changed the character of the city. As a result, London is now an exciting, **multicultural** city.

Some of London's Asian **immigrants** settled near Brick Lane market (above).

Industry

In the mid-1800s London became wealthy through trade with countries all over the world. People found work at the docks, loading goods for **export** and unloading goods for **import**. Some people found work in **manufacturing**, banking or medicine.

Many workers lived in rows of cheap houses, built closely together in order to provide shelter for as many people as possible. As more people moved in, some of these areas became **slums**. Later new homes were built away from the city. When public transport became available, many people moved to these new suburban areas and **commuted** to the city.

Docks on the River Thames bustled with activity in the early 20th century.

Children playing in a London slum.

As time passed, factories moved outside London. The companies that remained in the city managed the shipping of British goods around the world. Foreign banks moved their offices to London.

Between the 1960s and the 1980s London's port declined. At the same time, Britain's manufacturing industry declined, leaving many people unemployed. However, with London's large population and growing number of tourists, the city still needed many workers in transport, health care and entertainment. Today London is one of the world's most important **financial** centres.

In the 1980s part of London's docks was transformed into the Docklands.

Transport

London streets in 1900 looked very different from those same streets today. Back then, they bustled with pedestrians and **omnibuses**. Cars were rarely seen. To avoid the crowded streets, people used "steamers", or steam-powered ships, to travel on the River Thames.

People also travelled through London by rail. In 1863 the world's first underground railway system opened in London. The London Underground, or the tube, allowed passengers to avoid traffic on the busy streets by travelling through underground tunnels.

This 1902 photo shows frams omnibuses and pedestrians crossing Westminster Bridge.

Then and Now

Horse-drawn cab, 1884

Black cab, today

Today many forms of transport are used throughout London. Many people travel on London's red double-decker buses or in black cabs. Railways continue to serve thousands of daily **commuters**. Now the London Underground has more than 270 stations.

London has five airports. Heathrow is the largest airport and is one of the busiest in the world. More than 64 million passengers pass through it each year.

London is both historic and modern. The Tower of London, nearly 1,000 years old, shares the city with the London Eye, the world's largest observation wheel, which opened in 2000. Between them, these two London landmarks cover centuries of British history.

Thousands of double-decker buses travel around London.

11

New York
Small Island to Metropolis

In 1626 the Dutch bought the 21-kilometre-long island of Manhattan from a group of Native Americans. Dutch settlers named this island New Amsterdam. Later the Dutch surrendered the island to the British, who renamed it New York. In 1898 the surrounding areas called Queens, Brooklyn, Staten Island and the Bronx joined Manhattan to form New York City.

By 1900 thousands of **immigrants** were arriving daily to what was already the largest city in the United States. City planners began to work on providing more space in which people could work and live. Tall buildings were constructed to accommodate the city's workers. In 1902 the Flatiron Building was completed. It was the first of the many skyscrapers that would form Manhattan's skyline.

New Yorkers

By 1900 millions of people had **emigrated** to the United States, seeking the chance for a better life. The first stop for many immigrants who entered the country was New York. A large number stayed, helping to make New York a diverse, **multicultural** city.

Harlem has a large African-American population.

Over the years, thousands of African-Americans moved from southern states and settled in New York. Many lived in Harlem, a neighbourhood in northern Manhattan that became a centre of African-American literature, art, dance and music. Today African-Americans make up 25 per cent of New York's population. This cultural mix makes New York a **cosmopolitan** place.

Industry

In the 1900s New York was the headquarters for US industry. More ships passed through its port than through any other. Many factories were built near the port in order to ship goods overseas.

People became interested in the arts, and the entertainment industry thrived. A street that runs the length of Manhattan, called Broadway, became home to many theatres.

Broadway is the centre of New York's theatre district.

This photo shows Broadway in the early 20th century.

Today New York is the site of many banks and **financial** companies. It is also a leader in world business and finance. At the city's famous **stock exchanges**, stocks and bonds are bought and sold, or traded daily. New York is a cultural centre as well. Manhattan's clothing district continues to employ thousands of people. New York is also a major media centre where many books, magazines and newspapers are published. Radio and television stations and many top advertising agencies are based in the city. Lots of people are also employed in hotels, restaurants, galleries and museums to serve the public.

Then and Now

New York Stock Exchange, 1895

New York Stock Exchange, today

15

Transport

In the early 20th century New York's large population made transport a challenge. Horse-drawn carriages were crammed, and the streets were overcrowded. Planners built a raised railway, known as the "El", but its noise frightened horses, and cinders and soot fell onto the streets.

City planners decided to build underground instead. In 1904 the first 14 kilometres of tracks for the subway, or underground railway, were completed. Today New York has more than 1,125 kilometres of subway tracks and 450 stations. More than 3.5 million people travel on the subway every day.

Before the subway (above), the "El", or elevated train, took New Yorkers around the city.

New York's yellow cabs prepare for another busy day.

Above ground, cars eventually replaced horses and electric-powered streetcars. New roads and bridges were built so people could drive around the vast city more easily. Today there are sixty-five bridges and several tunnels linking different parts of the city. Ferries also carry **commuters** and tourists from one area to another. The city's famous yellow cabs, which first appeared in 1907, can be seen on almost every corner. Their honking horns is a trademark of the hustle and bustle of city life.

New York is known as the "Big Apple". With its diverse population, tall skyscrapers, vibrant cultural offerings and thriving **financial** district, New York is one of the world's greatest cities.

Toronto
"Meeting Place" to Thriving City

Toronto is found on Lake Ontario – one of the five Great Lakes in North America. Originally it was a French trading post, but by the late 1700s the area was a settlement occupied by the British. In 1834 the British named the city *Toronto* (a Native American word that means "meeting place").

Like London and New York, Toronto grew in size as people came in search of a better life. By 1900 it had railways, factories and a port. In 1904, however, a fire destroyed more than a hundred buildings. Out of these ruins, a new city developed. Skyscrapers were built, and Toronto's present skyline began to take shape.

In 1998 Toronto and the five communities surrounding it joined to form one city. It covers 630 square kilometres. Today Toronto is home to almost 5 million people.

Torontonians

Most of Toronto's early **immigrants** were British. After World War II, large numbers of immigrants from other countries arrived. They were encouraged to be loyal to their new land but also to preserve their culture – an idea known as "the Canadian mosaic". A mosaic is a picture or design made with many small pieces. Each piece has its own shape and colour, but is also part of a larger picture. As home to more than eighty **ethnic** groups and more than one hundred languages, Toronto is a big part of the Canadian mosaic.

Although there are some distinct communities such as Little Italy, Greektown, Little India and Chinatown, there are also neighbourhoods in which many different cultures live together. Today the fastest-growing immigrant groups are from Asian countries. These new Canadians have contributed to the culture, art, education and industrial development of the city.

Toronto's Chinatown has one of North America's largest Asian populations.

Lumber mills in northern Ontario helped Toronto become the city it is today.

Industry

From its beginnings as a centre for fur trading, Toronto has been an ideal location for business and trade. The opening of the Erie Canal and the building of railways led to rapid growth in industry. Lumber mills and tanneries, places where animal hides are made into leather, were built. Towards the end of the 19th century, commercial farming was expanding and timber was used to build cities and towns.

When gold, silver and other valuable minerals were discovered in northern Ontario, it had a big impact on Toronto. It helped the city develop as a centre for planning, financing and directing mining developments. Much of Toronto's mining helped supply industries in the United States.

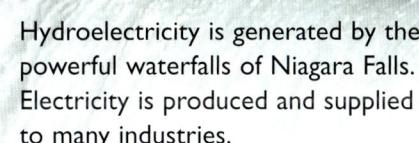

Hydroelectricity is generated by the powerful waterfalls of Niagara Falls. Electricity is produced and supplied to many industries.

The 1900s saw the growth of new industries. Electrical equipment, chemicals, cars, aluminium, pulp and paper, radios, home appliances and aircraft were all manufactured in Toronto. Many of these industries relied on cheap hydroelectric power supplied by Niagara Falls, which is 110 kilometres from the city.

Today Toronto provides a sixth of all jobs for Canadians. It is Canada's banking capital and the home of the Toronto **Stock Exchange**. Toronto is the printing and publishing centre of English-speaking Canada.

Recently many films and television shows have been made in Toronto, earning it the title, "Hollywood North". Toronto is also known for its food and beverage production, technology and pharmaceutical, or medicine, **manufacturing**.

Toronto stages a film festival every year.

21

Cars and electric trams carried passengers along Yonge Street.

Transport

At the beginning of the 20th century, Torontonians travelled from place to place by **omnibus**, electric tram or car. When the streets were covered with snow, people rode in horse-drawn sleighs. The city was also growing in importance as a railway centre. In 1964 Toronto and its surrounding areas became the first place to use a computer-controlled traffic system.

Today Toronto's highways wind in all directions. The city's modern transit system includes tram, bus and subway routes. This system connects residents and visitors to shopping centres, sporting and cultural events and the city centre. **Commuter** trains and buses bring people into the city from surrounding areas. Almost a quarter of city workers use public transport, but many prefer to drive. As in many large cities, traffic jams are frequent, and solving this problem is a challenge for city planners.

Toronto's road network is very large.

Then and Now

Toronto tram, 1908

Toronto tram, today

Despite its many challenges, this city by the water has a small-town friendliness. It's a place in which people of various cultures and backgrounds come together to create the Canadian mosaic.

23

Sydney
Convict Settlement to Olympic City

In 1770 Captain James Cook claimed the entire east coast of Australia for Britain, naming it New South Wales. Then in 1788 a fleet of ships carrying more than 1,000 people landed in Sydney Cove. Most of these people were convicts who were sent to Australia.

The convicts became Sydney's workforce. By the early 1800s some of them had been pardoned and given land to farm. In 1851 the discovery of gold in New South Wales attracted thousands of people to the area. In the years that followed, Sydney prospered. Advances in transport were made and the harbour city flourished. Almost 150 years later, Sydney was awarded the honour of hosting the 2000 Summer Olympic Games.

Sydneysiders

Sydney is home to the largest urban population of Australian **Aboriginal people**. Aboriginal people have lived in Australia for more than 50,000 years. The Eora people, Aboriginal Australians, were the first Sydneysiders. Much of the Aboriginal culture was destroyed when Europeans arrived in Australia. Today, however, Aboriginal Australians again proudly celebrate their culture through storytelling, dance and art.

Traditional Aboriginal culture is popular today with both tourists and Australians.

Many groups have contributed to Sydney's **multicultural** face. For more than 150 years Sydney's culture was influenced by European **immigrants**, particularly those from Britain. After World War II many immigrants came to Sydney from European countries such as Greece and Italy. In more recent times, people from Asian countries have contributed to Sydney's multicultural neighbourhoods, celebrations and restaurants.

25

Industry

The land around Sydney is rich in minerals and metals. Mining was responsible for much of Sydney's early growth. The gold rush in the 1850s brought great wealth, as well as more British and Irish **immigrants**, to the city. About the same time, coal mining grew dramatically with the discovery of rich new mines. Coal mining began in Australia in the 1790s, but production increased after these discoveries. By 1900 coal was being mined not far from Sydney in places such as Lithgow, Newcastle and the Illawarra district.

The gold rush of the 1850s was the first of many in Australia.

Australia Day activities on Sydney Harbour attract visitors from far and wide.

Today **manufacturing** is as important to Sydney's industry as mining. Sydney's factories produce everything from clothing to electronics. A large percentage of the nation's products are **exported** from Sydney's harbour.

Sydney is also one of Australia's most popular tourist destinations, and attracts 4 million visitors annually. Sydney is the headquarters for Australia's main **financial** companies and is a thriving centre for business and the arts. In addition Sydney and nearby areas in New South Wales are home to a number of research centres.

Then and Now

Sydney surfers, 1931   **Bondi Beach, today**

Transport

As early as 1850 Sydney planners knew that the city would have transport problems unless a bridge was constructed to connect the North Shore to the city centre, south of the harbour. Construction of the Sydney Harbour Bridge began in 1926, and it was officially opened eight years later. Today more than 150,000 vehicles cross the bridge daily, while large ships pass easily beneath it. In 1992 the Sydney Harbour Tunnel was built. This provides an alternative way to travel, linking the north and south of the city.

It took eight years to build the Sydney Harbour Bridge.

Once it was complete, the Sydney Harbour Bridge revolutionized transport across the city.

Driving in the city is a challenge. The road network is confusing, and traffic is often congested. Fortunately, Sydney has a well-developed public transport system. A rail network with double-decker carriages moves people to and from the central business district. A **monorail** runs along a scenic route through Sydney to Darling Harbour. It is mostly used by sightseers.

For more than a century, ferries have also been a practical method of transport across the harbour. Day or night, they can be seen crossing the water. They carry Sydneysiders to their jobs and bring tourists to the many places of interest around the harbour.

This photo shows the monorail leaving the city centre, with Sydney Tower in the background.

Sydney captured the world's attention when it hosted the 2000 Summer Olympics. Ships and aeroplanes with people from around the world arrived in Sydney. With its fascinating blend of ancient and modern culture, it is truly one of the world's greatest cities.

Harbour ferries provide a fast and scenic journey from the suburbs to the city.

Appendix   Fast Facts

	London	**New York**	**Toronto**	**Sydney**
Location	southeastern England, United Kingdom	New York State, United States	Ontario, Canada	New South Wales, Australia
Estimated Population, 2003 (Metropolitan Area)	7 million	9 million	5 million	4 million
Average January Temperature	4°C	0.5°C	−4.5°C	22.5°C
Average July Temperature	17°C	23°C	21.5°C	13°C
Average Annual Rainfall	76 cm	112 cm	81 cm	122 cm
Places to Visit	• British Museum • Buckingham Palace • London Eye • Tower of London • Westminster Abbey	• Central Park • Coney Island • Empire State Building • Metropolitan Museum of Art • Statue of Liberty	• CN Tower • Harbourfront • Ontario Science Centre • Royal Ontario Museum • SkyDome	• Manly Beach • Powerhouse Museum • Sydney Harbour Bridge • Sydney Opera House • Taronga Zoo

Glossary

Aboriginal people	of or relating to the first people of a country
commute	to travel to and from work each day
cosmopolitan	worldly, belonging to all parts of the world
emigrated	left one country or region to settle in another
ethnic	relating to races or large groups of people classed according to common traits or customs
export	to send goods from one country to another for sale and use
financial	of or relating to money resources
immigrants	people who move to a country to live
import	to bring in goods from another country for sale and use
manufacturing	the act of making something from raw materials
metropolis	the main city of a state, country or region
metropolitan area	an area made up of a large city and its surrounding cities and towns
monorail	a railway with a single rail serving as a track
multicultural	relating to a mix of several distinct cultures
omnibuses	large public buses, or historically, horse-drawn carriages
slums	parts of a city where many people, especially poor people, live in crowded, run-down conditions
stock exchanges	places where stocks and bonds are bought and sold

Index

Aboriginal people 25
art 13, 14, 19, 25, 27
bridges 10, 17, 28
business 6, 15, 20, 27, 29
Canadian mosaic 19, 23
cars 10, 11, 17, 21, 22
Erie Canal 20
factories 6, 9, 14, 18, 27
Flatiron Building 12
gold 20, 24, 26
immigrants 7, 12, 13, 19, 25, 26
industry 8–9, 14–15, 20–21, 26–27
London 4, 6–11, 18, 30
London Eye 11, 30
London Underground 10, 11
Londoners 7
Manhattan 12, 13, 14, 15
manufacturing 8, 9, 21, 27
mining 20, 26, 27
New York 4, 5, 12–17, 18, 30
New Yorkers 13
Niagara Falls 21

omnibuses 10, 22
population 4, 6, 7, 9, 13, 16, 17, 25, 30
port 6, 9, 14, 18
railways 10, 11, 16, 18, 20, 22, 29
SkyDome 30
skyscrapers 12, 17, 18
stock exchanges 15, 21
Sydney 4, 5, 24–29, 30
Sydney Harbour Bridge 28, 30
Sydneysiders 25, 29
Thames, River 6, 8, 10
Toronto 4, 5, 18–23, 30
Torontonians 19, 22
tourists 9, 17, 25, 27, 29
Tower of London 11, 30
transport 4, 8, 9, 10–11, 16–17, 22–23, 24, 28–29
underground railway (subway) 10, 11, 16, 23
World War II 7, 19